In Loving Memory

Rafael Robert Gaspar

1/4/1972 - 8/24/2004

Our heartfelt thanks to Allison and Garth for
this precious gift of your
talents, honoring Rafael's life and
capturing his remarkable spirit. The depth of
your friendship and love helps
immortalize his smile and
passion for life,
for which
we are eternally grateful.
~The Gaspars

Printed in the United States of America

First Edition, 2014
Limited Run

ISBN 978-0-9893591-9-1
The Rafael Gaspar Memorial Foundation
a 501c(3) non-profit organization
Austin, Texas 78737

www.RafaelGaspar.com
Rafaelito's Gift by Allison Fullam
Illustrated by Garth Beams

Designed by Chandra Gaspar Achberger
Typography: Scroobly, Traveling Typewriter, Chaparral Pro
Published by The Rafael Gaspar Memorial Foundation

Rafaelito's Gift

by his friend Alekona (Allison Fullam)

This book is dedicated to Rafael's nieces Jessica and Abby, nephew Atlas Rafael, and all the future generations of Gaspars. May you enjoy learning about your wonderful uncle and his adventures.

It's also dedicated to Jack, Baby Miles and their dad Tim. Many of the highlights of Rafael's life were shared with Tim.

With much love to Rafael for inspiring us to always smile and look for adventure in all we do. We love and miss you but know you are always nearby, in a rising sun or a glowing moon.

January 4th, 1972, was a cold day.

But, something magical was about to happen.

From the cold came a huge ray of light

that wrapped warmth around everyone.

Rafael Robert Gaspar

entered the world and was born to his

proud parents, Doris and Gui Gui.

They smiled at their baby,

and to their delight,

he smiled back.

As a young boy in Yonkers, Rafaelito dreamed of sailing his own boat, so...

He Built it.

He sailed it.

It sank.

He smiled.
He had been
captain of
his first
boat.

When he was a little older
Rafaelito traveled to Seattle,
Washington to see his uncle.
They were hiking on a
trail in the woods
when a huge lightning
storm blew in.

"Too dangerous
on the trail" said
Rafaelito's uncle,

"We'll have to 'bushwhack'
to get home fast!"

With that, they ran into the
deepest woods, and chopped a
trail straight home.

Rafaelito smiled,
"Bushwhacking!"
he cheered.

A few years later, Rafaelito
went to college in Cortland, NY.

One day a huge
blizzard covered the
town in snow.

Most people stayed inside
their warm houses.

Not Rafaelito! He said
to his friend Alekona,

"Let's go for a bike ride."
So they did.
This made Alekona smile
from ear to ear.
Rafaelito smiled too.

Rafaelito had always dreamed
of seeing the world.
He set off
to do just that.

First he went to Alaska
and got a job cleaning
Salmon with his buddy Tim.

This was the smelliest job he ever had.
Rafaelito never smelled anything so
horrible in his whole life!
But when he saw the piles
of clean fish from his hard work,
he smiled.

Rafaelito moved to Hawaii.

He fell in love with the sea.

He learned to surf.

He learned to fall.

He learned to
Get Back Up.

The salty air
made him
smile.

Rafaelito was exploring New York City, riding his bike and delivering messages to people.

One day, a yellow taxi-cab hit his bike. Rafaelito was okay.

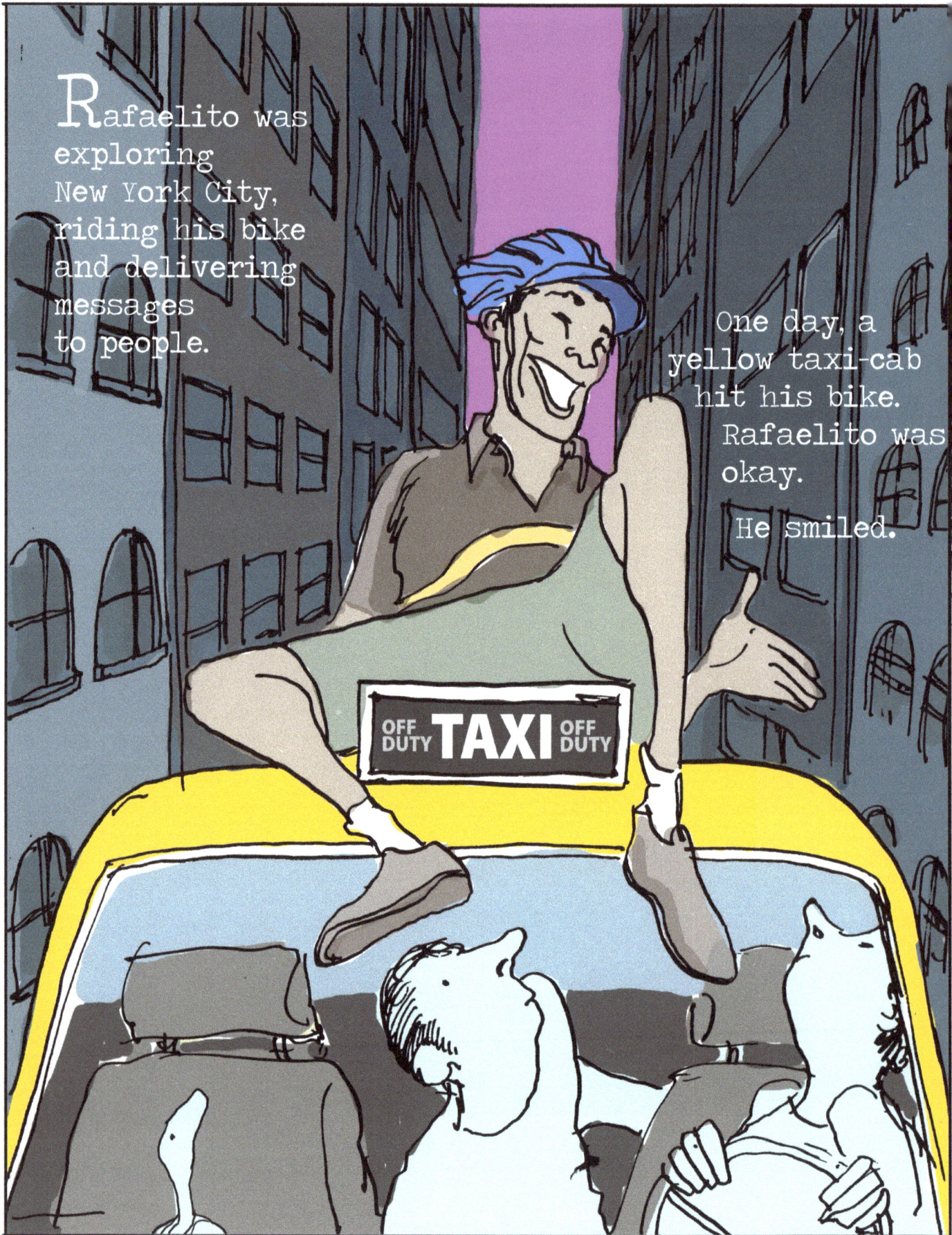

He smiled.

OFF DUTY **TAXI** OFF DUTY

After that,
Rafaelito went to
Indonesia. He saw his
first Komodo Dragon.
He was scared and then
excited.
Guess what?
Yup, he was still
smiling!

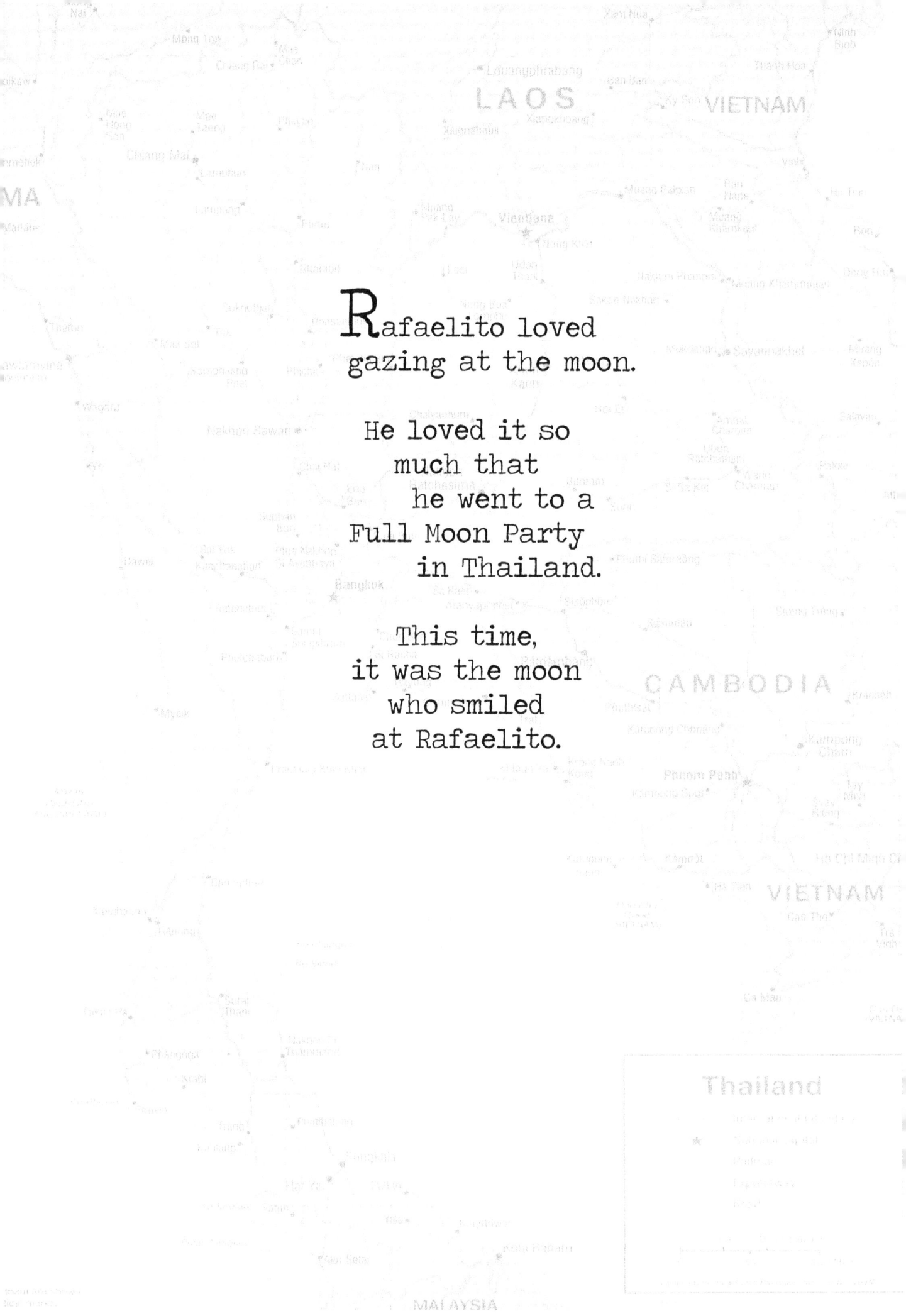

Rafaelito loved
gazing at the moon.

He loved it so
much that
he went to a
Full Moon Party
in Thailand.

This time,
it was the moon
who smiled
at Rafaelito.

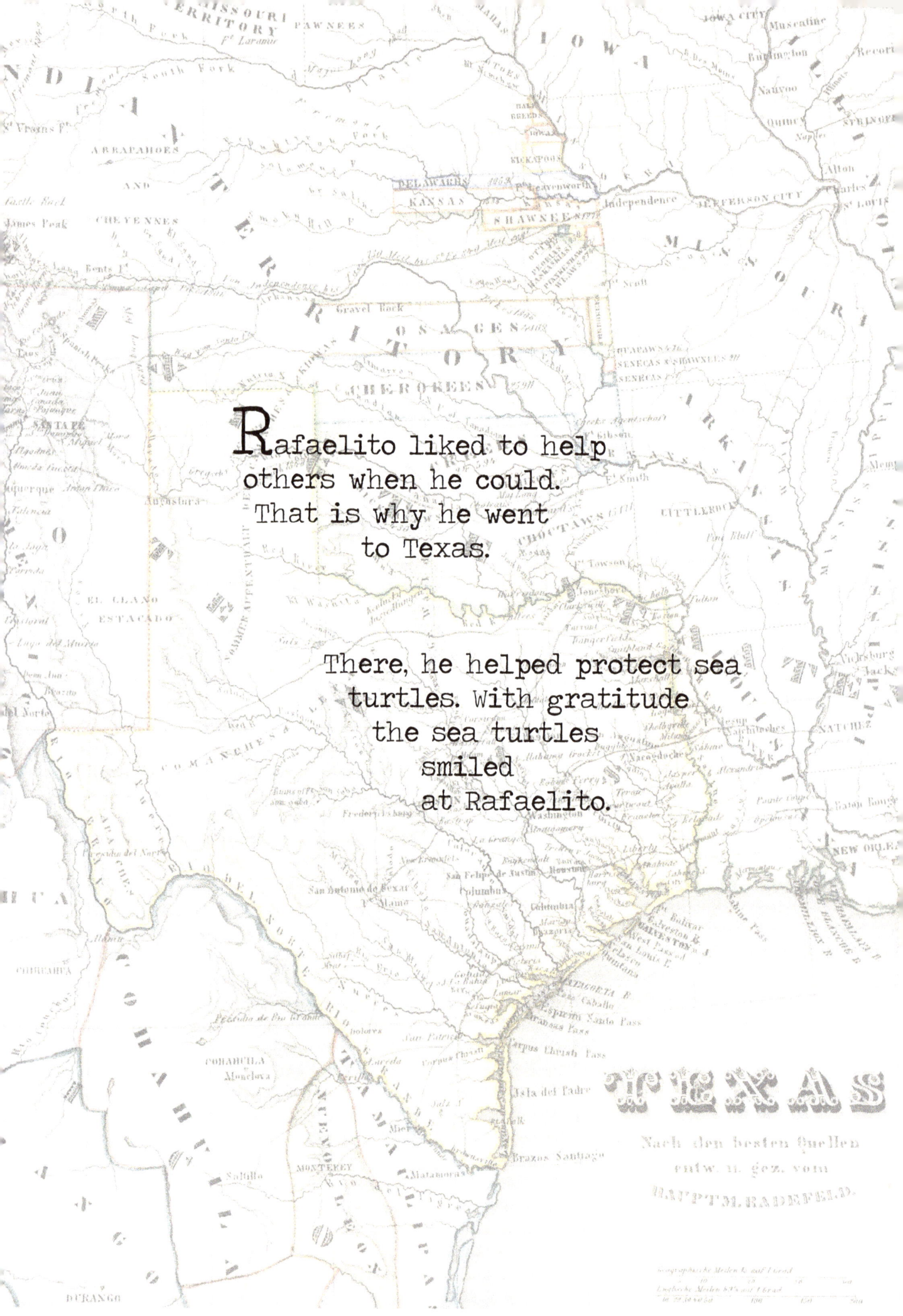

Rafaelito liked to help
others when he could.
That is why he went
to Texas.

There, he helped protect sea
turtles. With gratitude
the sea turtles
smiled
at Rafaelito.

Rafaelito still dreamed of being the
captain of his own boat, and when he got
to the Caribbean Sea,
he knew that he had found the
perfect spot.

So, he got a boat.
He learned to
sail it.

It didn't sink!
This made him
smile.

And it made all his
friends smile too!

Rafaelito carried his smile with him
on every one of his adventures.
And, if you look real closely,
you can see his smile
in the fish he met,
the ocean he surfed,
the moon he admired,
the turtles he helped,
the snow he played in,
and the sun he gazed upon.

But the best place to see
Rafaelito's smile
is in all the faces of
all those he smiled at.

Make your dreams real,
keep your feet moving
and ALWAYS, ALWAYS
keep smiling

www.ingramcontent.com/pod-product-compliance
Lightning Source LLC
Chambersburg PA
CBHW040258100426
42811CB00011B/1307